Unmapped Worlds

∞

David Chorlton

FUTURECYCLE PRESS

www.futurecycle.org

Cover artwork, "Above the Treeline," watercolor/pastel triptych by David Chorlton; author photo by Roberta Chorlton; cover and interior book design by Diane Kistner; Arno Pro text and titling

Library of Congress Control Number: 2021933006

Published by FutureCycle Press
Athens, Georgia, USA

ISBN 978-1-952593-15-4

With thanks to Roberta
for the many years together.
They were wonderful,
and I miss you.

Contents

Shepherds

With makeshift blankets thrown around
their shoulders, the shepherds turn
and walk toward the streaming light
that ripples through the clouds
at dusk. Each one

has an isolated patch
of grass and stone in the daylong sun,
a bladder to drink from
and a pocketful of toothpicks.
Their voices burned away

years ago leaving nothing but salt
on their lips. They were handsome for a day,
lissome in youth,
and made contracts with time:
good health in exchange
for looks. While their complexions

are massaged away by the light,
cheekbones support their faces
and for all the detours
taken by their bones, the flesh and skin
hold onto them, but with the sky

as a mirror, each sees himself a little
bit God as he sweeps
back a lock of hair from his brow.

The Octogenarians

The stubborn men refuse to have their jackets cleaned.
Bad luck, they say. A cold rain
climbs toward them from the valley.
Their village cuts into the sky

on its russet peak
where a few stone houses cluster
and the leaves fall first of any
in the country. The men
wear shirts whose collars curl at the yellow edges

and sweaters stained
with wine and butter. They have no one
to impress, no women to be gracious for,
and when they take their walking sticks

it is to scatter the chickens
that get in their way.
When the rain arrives, they let it run

into the creases on their skin
and wash the dust of summer out.
When others run
for shelter, they say it is too late

to go inside.
They love the mud.
It is the body
they are part of. Eighty years

was only a beginning
and one set of clothes
is enough for the rest.

The Sacristan

On sunny days the sacristan
scoops his shadow from the ground
and wraps it around
his skinny shoulders. In a country

whose plains flash light and dark
as clouds gather and burst
he leaves his footprints
in the mud but never
enters church without polishing

his shoes. When he traverses the square
at the center of his town,
his cloak flares.
Black is the only color

he wears. The curtains in his room
are thick as night
and his table is draped
in mourning cloth. He loathes
the light that penetrates the holy space

in which he works. When he breaks
bread, its heart
spills out as coal dust.

Wolf Boy

The wild boy from the stone house
was raised by wolves.
When his parents leave for the fields

it is still dark, and they do not return
until the moon
washes the roof with silver.
As soon as they know he is alone

the wolves come,
teaching the boy to move
on hands and knees,
and to let
the loud cries free

that are trapped in his throat.
He is a rumor
in inns and village squares,
the subject of reports in the press,

a miracle to some
and unnatural to others.
Only his parents

have no opinion.
They come home broken
by their labor and never see
the little flame of fear

in the boy's eye
as he watches them devour
their frugal meals.

Northern Midsummer

In all the colored houses
clustered by the lake
beside a gray mountain
girls are coming of age.
They refuse their Protestant suppers

and drift to the water,
listening for the one-string violin
that accompanies the cool

grassy scent of insomnia
rising around them
in endless daylight.
They are braiding their hair,

making wildflower chains
and wringing their hands as they watch
ancient wooden beds
float into the midnight sun.

Old Couple in a Storm

In the thunderstruck rooms of a barely furnished house
the owners sit on rough
cobbled chairs, gazing past each other

as lightning fires its white
shocks through them. For seconds
at a time they have electric faces,
ivory hands and sleeping caps

pulled down across chalk brows, then
they soak into the soft, dark walls

and as they grip their knees
the only light is from the bones
shining through the skin on their fingers.

The Cuckoo at the Border

A cuckoo who sings on a hidden branch
has laid her eggs among those
of a thrush. The money in our pockets changes
from currency to currency
when we walk through the forest
where darkness reserves are stored
for the resumption of hostilities
and the watchtower has been outlived by its shadow.

Still Time

Flies are airborne drops of honey
backlit in the windows
where the dust of summer drifts
into a room on the afternoon heat.
Exhaling old kisses as they sleep,
a husband and wife lie still
and dream of brandy
maturing in the fruit trees.

The Lamplighter in Prague

The only light I ever loved was gas. I sparked
the lamps at dusk and snuffed them out at dawn.
Craving shadows in the crooked lanes,
I slid between the darkness and the walls
of which I was a part, and from behind my face
I looked at passing lives as flames
spread a layer of secrets across them.
The city had more heart than I did then, before the electric
revolution when my skills burned like moths
in summer and I moved into the cellar
to remember how I kept a century from ending.

Bells

As bells peal for midnight from a hundred towers
in the rain, the amiable drunks going home
stop to listen with their faces tilted
like dishes positioned to catch the notes
as they fall. They spread their arms for balance
and never look down. The bell of Saint Nicholas
addresses them by name, saying it is time
to think of their wives already asleep, and the bell
of Saint Charles has a voice so deep it carries
all the way down to its brother metals in the earth.
Yes, it is late, says the old bell of Saint Ursula,
too late to turn back. Each of the drunks places
a finger at his lips and turns to the one beside him
with bubbles of laughter puffing out his cheeks.

Ice Cream

The ice bell rings
as the man from Morelia wheels
his continent through town
in a wagon the red of a midnight sun.
Here are the stars, he cries, *here
is the snow.* The snow with its tracks
of caribou, the snow with silence
packed inside it, the snow of which
a wedding dress is made. Here are drifts
of powder that cover the mountains
and veil the eyes of the Earth. Here
are day and night and cream. Listen to them
jangle, like a bracelet
with its frosty grip on a young lady's wrist.

Cabaret

When the spinsters rise in the night
to sip from their wide, white cups
they fold the sheets on their beds
as if creasing a letter
and tune their radios to the station
playing the same smoky songs
hour after hour, year after year.
How lonely the spotlight must be, they think,
how bitter the gin
that flavors the voice. And they float
across the moonlit floors
in their chrysanthemum gowns
from kiss to porcelain kiss.

Fairground

Silence has no home
like the fairground
when the fortune teller has washed
off her makeup, the ghost train
has made its last run,
the peep shows are dark,
the prizes nobody won
lie still in plastic wraps,

sleet begins to fall
and the guard makes his rounds
with his collar turned up,
listening to a pocket radio
play static

broadcast directly
from the afterlife.

Waiting Rooms

For the train without fear
of darkness, for the journey away
from the cold, for a seat
among the chosen, the passengers wait;

and for forgiveness, for the late departure,
the ticket inspector and confessor,
for fires to burn down in their cities
and for their sentences to be repealed.
They sit while the second hand
skirts the edge of the clock,
waiting for a place in the overcrowded carriage

with a suitcase full of ashes,
for a cure, for an end
to injustice, for the international
express, for the rain to stop,

and they wait with their eyes closed,
with half-eaten sandwiches
wrapped and saved for later,
with no reservations
and yesterday's newspapers crumpled unread.
They wait out of habit

with timetables in hand,
tired of war, of weak coffee
and of listening

for the voice in the loudspeaker
to announce the outbreak
of compassion and delayed arrivals.
Their patience is immeasurable

as the faith of heretics.

Tromp L'oeil

On the inner walls of a stone house
that holds by a claw to the slope
overlooking a vast bowl of trees
the prisoner, incarcerated with no tool but a brush,
made pictures of a storm,
believing he needed only create the sky
in order to fly away. When the walls
beat him back he covered them with the sea,
wide and dappled with sunlight,
and determined to swim
through them, but he flailed his arms in vain
until only plaster splashed around him
and he reached for his black paints
with which to depict the night.
Then he heard pines
groaning in the wind, the glass in the windows
rattling and, when he was alone,
the wolf sniffing at the door
he could not unlock. But there were always crusts
left over from supper
which he smuggled through the crack
above the step, and he pushed them on through
before he lay down to sleep
with his head on the pillow he had drawn
on the floor with the same chalk
he used to keep record of the days.

Every Day

Every morning the first bus leaves its depot
wiping the sleep from its headlamps;
a circle of blue flames ignites
beneath the kettle, a piece of fresh toast
hops on the hand
that takes it to the table
while the mint taste of toothpaste
bites through the furry residue
night has left in the mouth.
So it starts:

another day, another cartwheel of the clock,
another predictable page
in a book of hours. But once in a while
beside the plate a spoon is missing,
the keys are nowhere to be found,
a credit card disappears
into a slot that won't cough it back,
all flights

have been cancelled. The sky
is eerily quiet
and the birds' uninterrupted songs
would have us believe
this is a normal day.

One Minute to Midnight

A country lies waiting
for its trains to depart:
the ones at rest
in huge terminals
made of glass and steel
and longing
where passengers sip the night
from paper cups as they look
out along the tracks
stretching into moonlight.
They are many,
but bound together
by holding
one collective breath
as the time approaches
for them to leave,
each on a separate journey
one-way through sleep
flying close the ground
until sunrise. How quietly
they stand beside their luggage;
sentries at the gates
of someone else's life.

Teachers

The history teacher pulls a year
from his box of dates
and tells us to remember it.

The mathematics teacher tips numbers
onto the floor
and orders his favorite pupil
to sweep them up.

The music teacher plays a note
on the piano
and promises another tomorrow.

The art teacher brings flowers,
lead pencils and paper,
and tells the class
color is everything.

The English teacher chalks punctuation
marks on the blackboard
and leaves them for the French teacher
to use in the next lesson.

The divinity teacher describes God
but can't prove that He exists,
only points

to the black cloak above the school
where the headmaster flies
with a cane in his hand.

Emptying the House

Open the chest of drawers
and give the woolen vests back to the moths.
Release the handkerchiefs
from an outstretched hand
and watch them fly.
Hang the longjohns on the line
for them to kick back at the wind.

Stack the black discs
with Beethoven in their grooves
to make a tower of silence.
Keep the books with fragile bindings
whose sentences are a hundred years long
with breath for punctuation.

Treat the teapot as a trophy
for drinking fourteen cups a day.
Tap the pipe on the rim of the ashtray
until it coughs out the last
of its ashes.
Push the upright piano

outside and listen to the rain
improvise on its keys.

Perfection

With the Dutch precision of an old master
or the concentration of a tool
with no soul
perfection is possible. It may be
photographic realism
or an edge so sharp
it bleeds. It may be an aria
that flies, or a cadenza straight
from the subconscious fingers of a soloist
whose bow is strung with lightning.
For those who never come close
the consolation lies
in the journey; the lifelong meditation
or daily discipline
on the yoga mat as the limbs
become liquid and flow
through the poses without ever
moving far enough east
to slip through the knot
and leave the body behind.

The Mystic, Hildegard

Hildegard has a silkworm in her heart.
Her soul is thread.
Ecstasy is a tangle

and the worm spins a world
around the branches of her lungs.
Hildegard winds
silk on her transparent hands,

tightening the spirit
on the flesh. She is invisible,

having bound herself entirely
in the silkworm's joy.
Her skin is light.
She is a spiral

drilling the sky. The worm
works on. Even
small creatures must be fed,

and from the floating heart
it chews a daily ration.
The soul streams endlessly
within us, but silk

is our own flesh grinding
in the teeth of the mystery.

A Purple Vision of the Virgin

On the windswept rise
where Hildegard watches dawn

an adder slips beside her
like Adam's melting rib. She strokes

then gives it back
to the world beneath the soil. The sky

is purple as the early gale
leaps over hills and grips

the limbs of a tree whose leaves
ring against each other, sparkling

in the velvet light
while all the Earth is howling.

From the tree, Hildegard
hears a voice. When bark

falls away, the Virgin steps forward
and smiles

as she wipes a kiss of poison from her mouth.

Hildegard Receives a Messenger

An Italian messenger has crossed the Alps
carrying a scroll of news
from all the convents in the order. Hildegard
thinks his home is close

to the end of all mountains
where the messenger can see
almost to the lowest rung of Heaven.
This world

curls up at its edges, holding
seas back from infinity, she claims, and we
float in a sphere we cannot see.
The sphere in turn

is floating in an oval space
which fits inside
another, still another layer
away from the stars. This is a skin

of fire turning blue. As the messenger reads
a list of the departed, Hildegard
imagines their journeys: their bodies
growing light as the spirit

steps out of them
to climb invisible ladders
from universe to universe.

Hildegard's Vision

Never blinking, Hildegard
gazes at the parched
earth in July, wishing

she were a blade
of grass on the aching
hills. She faces
the sun until

her eyes evaporate
and light floods

the caves behind them.
In her skull
the wet walls turn
to steam. The snake

in her stomach uncoils
and slips into
a cooler skin

while Hildegard tears
her clothes. She pulls
the sky toward her.
The sun

is a swarm of bees.
She embraces
the buzzing fires

that carry her
to a bed of thorns and ice.

Life Addresses Hildegard

Three hours from daylight, dressing
for prayer, Hildegard
confronts a golden figure.
Life has locked the door

and blown out all the candles.
A voice is glowing in the cell:

I am a mirror among stars,
the stone at the core of the sun,
the wind's tongue,
the nettles in your skin.
I have framed your face in leaves
and planted bindweed in your womb.

Hildegard steels her cheek
but Life merely
runs a parting finger there
and enters the coiling smoke.

Bertran de Born

(1140–1215)

Bertran loves the sway
of the spine beneath him, the mane
and colors streaming,
the forest singing
as he shines between the foliage

in April when he wakes
and freshens his complexion.
The finches tell him it is time

to delight in the swing
of an iron ball
against a neighbor's armor
and to watch him fall
into the lavender.
When fires blossom

he carries home his verses
of blood and columbine
to show lovers of fine words

that poetry is strongest
when written with an arrow
on the breast of his opponent.

Bruegel's Glass

On the last day of the Middle Ages
Pieter Bruegel takes inventory
and raises a glass
to his eye

better to see the myriad faces
in their pallor
as body and soul peel apart
releasing a fine mist
that tastes of apples and sulfur.
It was an elegant time

when voices rose in sonic cathedrals,
clothes were a brilliance
and poetry was spun in lines of silk

as long as the breath
a singer could draw. It was a festive time
when banners crackled
in a whiplash of light and the sleeves
of the rich were swollen

with color; a time of barren dunes
whose counterpoint was fire
and of towers pricking an icy sky.
Unrecorded is the view

the victims have when they look back
at their painter: a stubble-chinned man
just plying his craft,

reducing Hell to a hoofbeat
and Heaven to a flake of snow
melting at a touch.

A Letter from the New World

Our ship was a basket of lights
on the ocean. For Saint James' Day
we hung a hundred lanterns
and ate the last dry meat,
then had to live

on rats and peppers.
Boys chanted prayers
and mysteries, all the hours

and passing days. We sat
with our pots of seed, beating
down the roaches while
we talked about soil. Men
painted red

greeted us with strange food
at the first island. Before
we crossed the Gulf
a friar drinking chocolate

was struck cold by an arrow.
He died at sea. The deck
was rattling when we threw him
into the largest grave

a man can have. Finally
we stepped onto the world beyond
all others, where the land
belongs to those who claim it.

The Final Battle for Tenochtitlan

In a city built of marble and feathers,
stones fall in sheets
and priests run with their hair
like roosters' crests, crimson
with old blood. As dust

beats down the fires, Moctezuma
rolls a jaguar skull in his hands,
fingering the blue rocks
planted there. Imagining jugglers

in the streets, he calls for his canopy
of blinding green, a necklace
of live birds, and a bath filled with pearls.
He offers his aviaries
for peace and tears the gems
from his sandals

but everything that Spaniards want
they take. Arriving with a string of beads,
they traded an empire
for musk-scented glass, and claim
the markets, tobacco
and fountains. They will possess

all they destroy.
Hearts glow
on clay altars in the temple,
beating on the gentle coals

while the next god waits
with gunpowder and chiles
enough to survive. As they crumble,
the defenders cry:

Whether for us or for yourselves
you will rebuild this city.

Desert Baroque

While sleeping in their cells
the Fathers threw off the sheets
to roll from dream to dream
with transatlantic salt gleaming
on their unwashed skins

and their faith preserved in the frost
of the other world.
They pledged their skulls to this land
with tranquility in its thorns,
redesigned the sky
to accommodate a god
who spoke to them in Latin

and hung bells to give the wind
a Latin voice, but it licked the metal
and carried a bitter taste
into canyons too deep
to convert. They built shadows

with mud, carved them
for birds to nest in the scrolls
they engraved in the clouds
into which they disappeared

at the end of the looping script
in their letters, subsequently rolled
to resemble their bones
and carried away on a tired horse.

Relics

The empty habit of a priest
appears between Heaven and Earth
with the cross on a string of beads
still flowering on the breast.

His sandals, alight with needles,
rest on the incline
where he stepped out of his body,
and red blossoms have grown
at the nine tips of his whip
that put down roots since last
it stung his back.

The shadow of his horizontal arms
is burned into the pale stones
where he was nailed
to the heat

and the bones he left behind
withered into straws
which were taken for a nest
by the immortal Phainopepla.

Pimeria Alta (II)

A flash flood of light came over the horizon
and washed the creosote
until it was white as the face of the priest
who knelt in an arroyo
with his hands held open to receive it.
The prayer on his lips turned to smoke

as an aura appeared around each of the flowers
for which he had no name
and the first wave of light touched his robe
which turned the orange of the blooms
on the barrel cactus. Faces blossomed
on stalks of agave. Flycatchers swooped

and drew ornaments on pages of air. He leaned back
against an updraft of wind
and turned his eyes
toward the sky as it folded around him.
A needle entered his heart
so gently he smiled.

Pimeria Alta (IX)

Each with his or her own belief, each with the comfort
the stars bring, and each with the balm
the cool air brings after darkness,
the mission's people breathe deeply as they dream
whatever the light denies them
when it hits with summer's force. The owl

from the tall saguaro, the coyote
from the mesquite trees, and a frog in the mud
at river's edge call, each to another
of its own kind. On the open page

to the gospels lying beside the priest's bed
a moth has settled with its wings open,
a bookmark from the spirits
of whom it is forbidden to speak.

The Jaroslavl Fresco

A likeness of God stares through the plaster.
At twilight he turns into a wolf.
His eyes are close together
and the pupils float on luminous globes.
Hair covers all
but the cheekbones

pushing against a patch of sallow skin.
It grows thicker by the century,
wild from its roots

to the frost on the tips
when he runs in moonlight
through the silent forest

with a star of blood
shining from prey in his teeth.

John Donne's Flea

Poetry fell on rosebuds
while the public squares
became theaters
in which a thief was marked
with fire on his hand
so as never to be shown again
a sign of mercy.
Next to apples in the marketplace
torturers displayed
their craft, and at the docks
the souls of prisoners set sail
for eternity. The age of viols,
lutes, and madrigals
was the age of women
broken on the wheel
one limb at a time. With all the devotion
of offering a prayer, the executioner
set to work on unbelievers
with a saw, dividing their inverted,
faithless bodies with a line
through consciousness and sleep.
The pear and iron maiden
flourished parallel
to the quill
that spoke with elegance,
and when John Donne's flea
drank blood, it was
nought but a drop
of love.

Silk

Silk is the far side of the Tigris,
half a year
across Asia, beyond

the elephants' homeland.
It rustles in the room
where an emperor sleeps

and lines serpentine tombs
under the sand.
Silk plains

are covered with bones.
Torn silk
marks borders all the way

from the ceramic gates to a city
afloat in palm groves
to the Chinese Wall. The steppes

are expanses of burnt silk,
black beneath the wind
guiding travelers

through the narrows
between Heaven and Earth
to the mulberry

where silkworms spin a continent
to spread
before the dark ambassadors

from the other end
of the unmapped world.

Canton, a Day in 1870

The Mandarin lives in a theater of peacock feathers,
rugs and wilting leaves. His children
hardly breathe. His wife

has a face of chalk and polished hair.
They live between poses
while dying has no ritual.
Gentlemen in symmetry

sit at tables with their cups
of formal tea. The crowds
attending punishments have been torn from the streets.
The Mandarin loves trinkets
and discipline. A smile

floats across his lips for strangers.
Four robbers kneel in the grass.
Even children watch.
The sky is porcelain

with a few blue strokes
for trees still holding
to the Earth. As the heads are swept away

the spectators return to the steam
from their meals. It is their way.
But one of them, a man in yellow slippers,
is laughing in the silent breeze.

The Vertical Desert

Broken layers of earth stand on their edges
with an age of thirst
pressed tight between sand
and the white stones ground
by a thousand-year wind
that dried everything

except the river
flowing through an eye in the skull
of a javelina
who burrowed

into silt to find shade
and slept until the juniper
rooted in his skin.

From Pueblo Grande

We cannot place the country
underneath us, although its stories
still carry on the red winds
bringing home the past
in a storm.

The land once had a color,
the sun was its clock
and calendar, vegetation a wealth
of detail running
across the valley, rooted
in brief rain.

This was all
before the city, in time
before time, when travelers from the coast
left shells here, while water
came at its own

slow pace, one drop
at a time, one river
in the whole world.

The Sound of People Disappearing

When, far from cities, the radio signal
turns to static and you stop
along the highway
and listen instead
to the darkness,
you can hear
the sound of people disappearing.
Their footsteps
are all around you.
When they speak
you cannot tune your ears
to their alphabet.
Their long skirts brush
against the drought
and air passes through their lungs
in slow breaths
you think to be your own.
If you remain still
enough to forget
where you intended to go
you will discern,
between nocturnal cries
from animals,
the smooth strokes of a straw comb
in a man's long hair.

A Bone

Calcium shadows
run through the caves
inside a vertebra
found on the desert
where it lay, stripped clean
and separated
from the others in its chain
that used to dip
and sway along a creature's back.
I keep it for the form,
for the dry weight
in my hand
when I turn it around
to feel the broken symmetry
where the honeycomb darkness
appears through a crack.
It was white
in the sun, pushing
its way between stones
as if the animal
could be reassembled
bone by bone. It fit
into the landscape,
part ghost, part monument,
and on those days
heat takes hold so tightly
we hallucinate
I pick it up
and wind my fingers
into the crevices
to experience the indestructible
shape of thirst.

Stones

The music in stones
is from particles grinding
at their centers, where
static plays its continuous succession
of consonants only
lizards can hear as they hold
onto stones the way rain
grips the glass desert.

Cicada Fire

The sky in the east turns silver
for a second, then becomes
dust again.
Cicadas pour themselves back

into last year's shells,
empty for months in sheltered
garden corners, and tune

themselves for a shrill
summer. They are an army
of musical clocks
whose wheels

grind sand and spark
a storm of storms

chain-reacting
inside every one
where the springs
melt down in the furnace.

Los Hermanos Hernandez

I   *January 22nd, 1933*

Three miles from Casa Grande
Charles Washburn sets a fire
beneath his coffee.
Manuel Hernandez

approaches him in English
while his brother Federico
is a shadow at his back.
The old man came from California

to look for gold;
now his car in the arroyo
cannot climb back to the road.
Federico lays the steel rod down

and Manuel his gun.
At the bottom of a well
Charles Washburn holds a Christmas card
beneath an inch of dirt.

Manuel gives Federico
ten dollars in the dark
and puts twenty in his pocket

three miles from Casa Grande,
an empty bottle in his hand.

II

Two men guilty of a single crime
are sentenced not to hang
but to inhale
and die with the fumes at sunrise
turning purple in their lungs.

III   *July 6th, 1934*

Watermelon rinds
surround the table like spent shells.

Eighteen kisses later
the boys watch their mother
hang a woven blanket
on the horns of the moon.

She turns back at the prison gate
where a Spanish prayer is smoke
coiling out from Manuel's lips

until he stands up to her weeping
and lights a man's cigar.
While the youngest sleep
on the prison lawn
adults pace on gravel

and a woman's wailing blanches
the walls of every cell.

IV

Manuel and Federico
climb the iron steps
and sit in the straight-backed chairs
with stethoscopes sucking

at the skin on their chests
and cotton gauze across their eyes.
The kit fox and coyote
lying down to sleep

raise their ears when Manuel's voice
flies over them at dawn
to appeal for Federico.
Five o'clock; the string

is cut, the fifteen pellets
fall, the gas spreads its fingers
and pulls them down together
into the water and the acid

with Manuel still talking
and Federico white.
Then the vacuum and the blowers

clean every trace of dying
and the witnesses away.

From Interstate 10

Sacred datura
gulp the roadside breeze.
We would have ninety-five

degrees in the shade
if there were any shade,
but light bounces off
asphalt at the speed limit.
To either side

the ground is dry enough to blow away
with yellow dusted
palo verde and smoky
blossomed trees

all the way to the crooked mountains.
Crosses lean
over desert graves

as if their roots could not hold them.
The earth is for sale
and the sky has been leased
a billboard at a time
for rich men's graffiti.
The border

is a hundred miles away
but official cars patrol it,
pulling over

errant vehicles
whose drivers are looking
for irrigation
in a land of air-conditioned souls.

Phoenix

after Cavafy

The road to Phoenix will lead you
through a landscape of illusions, where the rocks
are soft and molded by the wind,
where columns of dust hold up the sky,
and should you see somebody driving toward you
they will appear to float above the asphalt
as if the sun had lifted them. Signposts
will point to cultures you believed to be extinct:
cultures of patience and indifference
to your passing. If your hopes remain high
that Phoenix will offer you comfort and a future
better than your past, if you carry all you own,
if you have resolved to continue, unfold
another square of the map and reassure yourself
that Phoenix exists. Allow yourself
to look around at the stones emerging from the earth
and stop occasionally to feel the heat
hold you close and gradually eradicate
everything you leave behind. You may cease
believing in Phoenix, but travel on in faith.
If the days spent on the road seem never to end,
if they turn into months, even years, do not fear
the time is spent in vain. Hurrying is futile.
The distance to Phoenix is not measured in miles;
neither is speed of any importance.
The city will appear in its own time. Forget
why you set out for Phoenix and be content
with the wide open country that burns itself
into your eyes. This is the wealth
that impels you. Had there never been a Phoenix
you would not have seen the strata of rock laid bare
millennia ago, and neither the Phainopepla
nor the White-winged dove. Without Phoenix

none of what you see exists. If you arrive at last,
disappointed with what meets you,
you will be changed, and even if you have no strength
to turn around and go back to where you came from,
be content to know
that Phoenix cannot take your journey from you.

Subject for Study

"…the use of animal models constitutes
conceptual nonsense. Humans are the only
proper subjects for studies which aim to
elucidate human psychology."
                        —Murray Cohen, M.D.

The macaque would not tell us
what we need to know.
We shall return you to your life
if you still want to go there
once our records are complete.
First we cut a window

in your skull,
then thread these wires
to measure the pulse in your thoughts
as you accept your situation.
Have you taken amphetamines before?
Try to relax.
This is for the common good.
Are you used to being alone?
Does it make you cry?

Do the squealing cats disturb you?
Do you have one at home?
What is its name?
What is your name?

Stress is a problem for many people
who appreciate your help.
Would you like a cigarette?
Are the restraints too tight?

Think of your body as a harp
strung with nerves. Look at these pictures
from the Middle Ages; wasn't the Inquisition
a terrible waste with all its wheels and wooden racks?

When you sign the papers
confirming your compliance with our work
your soul shall be returned to you.
There it is, the cloud in the two-liter jar.

Citizenship Test

How far into the Earth does a country extend?
Is the temperature at the core
one hundred or twelve thousand degrees?
What is the melting point of a border?

If the stratosphere were occupied by a foreign power,
could we still breathe?
Do you feel as patriotic in the clouds
as you do on the ground?
Do you love your native steam?

How long did it take the European starlings
to reach California after arriving in New York:
forty years or forty thousand?
Does it take forty years to become American?
Does it help to have a certain plumage?

Is the collective weight of insects in America
greater than that of the humans?
What would happen if the humans weighed more?
Who would pollinate the flowers?
Are insects protected under the Constitution?

Is the country two hundred
or two hundred million years old?
When the continent shifts six inches in a year,
do you feel displaced?

Do you consider starlings a nuisance?
Is a future guaranteed?
Will the insects survive us?

Far North

The far north is waiting
for the wind to begin, for the blue
of its sky to slip under
clear water, for the edge
of its icebergs to slice
open the light
that sweeps over the slopes
of the mountains to change them
from azure to rose. The caribou drawn
on the haze lift their heads
and turn round, so massively slow
as to rattle the bones in their necks
while tracks mark the passage
of bears to the glow
of their den. In the far northern dusk
the air sharpens its teeth
on a stone. It is waiting
for someone to call the sun down
to its bed in the frost, for you
who are lost
to continue the journey
through time, to the valley where future
and past flow together
with no way to tell them apart.

Whisper

A whisper moves through the forest
while foxes stalk the darkness
with their fur hearts quietly beating.
It passes from tree to tree

like the tip of a cigarette
lighting the next in a chain
for smokers with nothing to do
but wait. It resembles the sound
of a page turning

or the static
from Radio Universe
broadcasting mystery

to those who cannot sleep.
And the syllable continues
to rustle, white against white,
fear against hope.

Survivor

When a man who has walked all day across desert finally stops to drink, the water breaks open like a flower in the pit of his stomach. Even from its lowest point in the sky, the sun bores through his skin. He touches himself to confirm that he has not evaporated during his journey and surveys the terrain he has crossed, where the surface appears undisturbed by his passing, wondering who disappeared there in his place.

Salesman

The salesman says he wants to make a deal, states a price and winks to let you know everything is negotiable. A tiny lightbulb on his tie is flashing as he speaks, and you cannot keep your eyes off it. On a notepad he begins to calculate how much you have to pay, then holds it up for you to see, and the buzzer goes off in the button he presses with his free hand under his lapel. This is it, he tells you: the bargain you have lived your life for, and he pulls paper streamers from his cuff. You are still undecided. The salesman takes the handkerchief from his pocket and flicks it to send a shower of confetti over you just as he begins to beat together the cymbals he has strapped to his knees. Why does it take you so long to consider his terms? He lies down on the floor and asks you to walk over him. Yes; do it. Wear pointed shoes; he will not let you know when you are hurting him. Do whatever you want, this is only his job.

The Cinema

Snow falls through the open roof of a bombed-out cinema in a city at the end of a war. A few seats have survived intact, and a beam of light shines from the projection room to the screen, where a sepia moving picture shows people walking through the streets. The snowflakes cast shadows on the screen. Several people sit huddled in their coats, pulling scarves around their faces and blowing into their hands. There is no sound to the film they are watching; it is so quiet they can hear the footsteps of the walkers in the street outside crunching snow, and in the distance the quickened breath of someone running. The film continues, slow, monotonous, and true to the scene outside, but the audience members endure it as long as they can look up and see the snowflakes bristling white as they pass through the projection beam.

Bees

The bees are coming. Nothing can stop them. There so many, we cannot hide from them. No lotions repel them. Their droning over-powers every other sound. They come in a heat wave, directly from the sun: golden fire, sunflowers exploding, lovesick soldiers wanting only to rub their yellow fur against our cheeks.

Television

When one stranger stops another in the street to ask the time, what he means is, *How many minutes do we have until the end times?* The one with a wristwatch peels back his sleeve and says *One million three hundred thousand four hundred and fifty-seven.* Overhearing the conversation, a third person stops and corrects him. *Five thousand two hundred and six.* An argument breaks out. A fourth person approaches, curious about the cause of the disagreement. *I heard nine hundred thousand two hundred and seventy-four,* he says, *but that was on the morning news and nobody can believe what is on television.* Then they all start talking about last night's programming. *I watched the show in which people eat live scorpions,* another responds, *and enjoyed it.* The others want to know whether there were condiments involved. *Yes, Tabasco sauce.* And the tips of the minute hands on all the watches glow where the stings taper to a point.

Free Sample

Opening the sachet, the recipient inhales the scent and studies the picture on the label of a crepuscular scene suggestive of a meeting place for good and evil. She reaches out to steady herself, but there is nothing to hold onto and she feels herself losing control, growing wings, letting herself be taken by the air. There she goes, where she has never been before, and now she is a Bird of Paradise perched on the lintel with her yellow crown and green throat sparkling, and her wings spread wide and fluttering like all the dresses she ever threw away.

The Mask

Tragedy's mask hangs on a rusty nail, its features melting and its skin worn thin by too much use. Through the eyeholes one can see lost empires, crows descending onto battlefields, and the wildflowers that grow over them. A cigarette sticks to a corner of its mouth with enough tobacco left for a few more drags. It can be stretched to fit any face. It sometimes seems to speak, but never in the bold way generals do. *For centuries, it says, we listened to the glorious speeches designed to make our pulses fast with pride as we raced to defend a high ideal and insult death, but death deceived us. It does not come charging draped in colors, but steals into our homes like the cleaning woman and leaves everything polished to a dazzling sheen.*

The Wolves

Let us journey to that country at the treeline whose people hold their banners high to honor a deity lost in the ancient snows from which even gods never return. Let us wear the local costumes and trade centuries of violence for a day of such peace even the wolves, wracked with hunger and cold as the stars, find the patience to wait for a blessing.

Acknowledgments

Grateful thanks to the editors of the publications in which these poems first appeared:

Abbey: "Teachers," "A Letter from the New World"
Amethyst Review: "Perfection"
Apocalypse: "The Sound of People Disappearing"
as it ought to be: "Relics," "The Jaroslavl Fresco"
Aura: "Wolf Boy," "Northern Midsummer"
Blakelight: "Desert Baroque"
Chiron Review: "John Donne's Flea"
Cholla Needles: "Stones," "Whisper"
Circle Show: "The Cuckoo at the Border," "A Bone"
Cumberland Poetry Review: "Old Couple in a Storm"
Dog River Review: "The Cinema"
International Poetry Review: "Pimeria Alta (IX)"
International Times: "Subject for Study," "Salesman," "Television"
January Review: "The Final Battle for Tenochtitlan," "Silk," "Cicada Fire"
Neologism: "Fairground"
New Laurel Review: "Canton, a Day in 1870"
Nexus: "The Mystic, Hildegard"
The Peacock Journal: "Still Time," "Bells," "Cabaret"
Poem: "Shepherds," "The Octogenarians," "The Sacristan," "Bruegel's Glass," "The Vertical Desert"
San Pedro River Review: "The Lamplighter in Prague," "Waiting Rooms," "From Interstate 10"
Skidrow Penthouse: "Pimeria Alta (II)," "Citizenship Test"
Slipstream: "Los Hermanos Hernandez," "Far North," "Survivor"
Third Wednesday: "Tromp L'oeil," "Every Day," "One Minute to Midnight"
Treehouse: "Emptying the House"
Verse-Virtual: "A Purple Vision of the Virgin," "Hildegard Receives a Messenger," "Hildegard's Vision," "Life Addresses Hildegard"
Visitant: "Bees," "Free Sample," "The Mask," "The Wolves"
Voices on the Wind: "Ice Cream," "Bertran de Born," "Phoenix"

About FutureCycle Press

FutureCycle Press is dedicated to publishing lasting English-language poetry in both print-on-demand and Kindle (digital eBook) formats. Founded in 2007 by long-time independent editor/publishers and partners Diane Kistner and Robert S. King, the press incorporated as a nonprofit in 2012. A number of our editors are distinguished poets and writers in their own right, and we have been actively involved in the small press movement going back to the early seventies.

We award the FutureCycle Poetry Book Prize and honorarium annually for the best full-length volume of poetry we published that year. Introduced in 2013, proceeds from our Good Works projects are donated to charity. Our Selected Poems series highlights contemporary poets with a substantial body of work to their credit; with this series we strive to resurrect work that has had limited distribution and is now out of print.

We are dedicated to giving all of the authors we publish the care their work deserves, offering a catalog of the most diverse and distinguished work possible, and paying forward any earnings to fund more great books. All of our books are kept "alive" and available unless and until an author requests a title be taken out of print.

We've learned a few things about independent publishing over the years. We've also evolved a unique and resilient publishing model that allows us to focus mainly on vetting and preserving for posterity poetry collections of exceptional quality without becoming overwhelmed with bookkeeping and mailing, fundraising activities, or taxing editorial and production "bubbles." To find out more about what we are doing, come see us at www.futurecycle.org.

The FutureCycle Poetry Book Prize

All full-length volumes of poetry published by FutureCycle Press in a given calendar year are considered for the annual FutureCycle Poetry Book Prize. This allows us to consider each submission on its own merits, outside of the context of a traditional contest. Too, the judges see the finished book, which will have benefitted from the beautiful book design and strong editorial gloss we are famous for.

The book ranked the best in judging is announced as the prize-winner in the subsequent year. There is no fixed monetary award; instead, the winning poet receives an honorarium of 20% of the total net royalties from all poetry books and chapbooks the press sold online in the year the winning book was published. The winner is also accorded the honor of being on the panel of judges for the next year's competition; all judges receive copies of all contending books to keep for their personal library.

www.ingramcontent.com/pod-product-compliance
Lightning Source LLC
Chambersburg PA
CBHW070011100426
42741CB00012B/3193